MAX SHEPHERD-CROSS

Our Flexible Future

Copyright © 2023 by Max Shepherd-Cross

All rights reserved. No part of this publication may be reproduced, stored or transmitted in any form or by any means, electronic, mechanical, photocopying, recording, scanning, or otherwise without written permission from the publisher. It is illegal to copy this book, post it to a website, or distribute it by any other means without permission.

First edition

This book was professionally typeset on Reedsy. Find out more at reedsy.com

Contents

Introduction	1
Flexibility is More than a Trend	3
The Freedom of Choice - Unpacking the Modern Workspace	6
The Business Sense Behind Letting Employees Choose Their...	9
Visibility: The Foundation of Effective Flexibility	13
Flexibility is Not Chaos	19
Why Office Mandates Don't Work	22
Data-Driven Insights Amplify Flexibility's Potential	28
Managing Employees in a Flexible Workplace	31
The Path Forward with Flexibility at its Core	34

Introduction

Choice – that's the new cornerstone of our work world. The freedom to decide where we set up our laptops, whether it's a sunlit home office, a bustling cafe, or that cozy corner spot at the company headquarters. The potential of this choice-based workspace is exciting: widening the talent pool, fostering autonomy, and offering a tailored work environment that suits each individual.

Yet, with such freedom comes its own set of challenges. How do we keep connected when our team is dispersed? How can businesses ensure their spaces cater to this dynamic work approach? And more fundamentally, how do employees best choose their workspace wisely each day?

When executed correctly, this shift toward choice-driven workspaces can be a game changer. It has enabled companies like Airbnb and Atlassian to tap into a global talent pool, nurturing autonomy and generating a sense of ownership among their employees. Allowing for a work environment that's as unique as the people who make up the team, increasing overall job satisfaction and productivity.

However, the freedom to choose comes with its own unique challenges. A lack of coordination can lead to disconnected teams, a less cohesive company culture, and underutilized office spaces. Companies such as Amazon and Starbucks have seen employees revolt against their mandated office days. Poorly managed, it can lead to operational inefficiencies, increased costs, and could even turn into a competitive disadvantage. In the worst-case scenario, you might face employee disengagement and turnover, eroding the very benefits that flexible work promises.

Here at Officely, we've been at the forefront of this shift, understanding its intricacies and paving the way for choice-driven workspaces. This guide is your toolkit. We'll break down the allure of workspace freedom, face its challenges head-on, and provide a blueprint to make flexible work, really work.

Join us as we explore the landscape of choice in the modern workspace and unlock its vast possibilities.

Flexibility is More than a Trend

The Historical Context: Evolution of the Workspace

The workspace has always been in flux, moulding itself to societal needs, technological advancements, and global trends. The move towards flexibility isn't just another passing fad; it's a reflection of our evolutionary trajectory.

From open-plan offices aiming to foster collaboration in the late 20th century to the rise of coworking spaces in the early 21st century, our work environments have continuously adapted. The demand for flexibility is the next logical step, tapping into our innate need for autonomy, balance, and efficiency.

As early as the 1970s, futurists predicted the rise of 'satellite offices' – decentralized hubs allowing for better work-life balance. Fast forward to today, and we're living that reality.

The Global Catalyst: Remote Work Surges

Recent global events, particularly the pandemic, acted as a catalyst, urging organizations to consider remote and flexible options. This wasn't just a reaction to the crisis but a realization of the potential inherent in flexible models.

While circumstances necessitated the shift, many organizations found unexpected benefits. Teams remained productive, overheads reduced, and employees reported higher job satisfaction. This forced experiment demonstrated that flexibility wasn't just feasible but, in many cases, preferable.

Beyond Work-Life Balance: The New Work-Life Integration

"Work-Life Balance" was the catchphrase of the 2000s. Today, it's evolved into "Work-Life Integration," where work and life don't compete but coexist harmoniously.

Flexibility supports this seamless integration. It recognizes that employees aren't just workers but human beings with varied responsibilities, interests, and aspirations. The beauty of flexibility lies in its adaptability, allowing work to fit into life and not the other way around.

Encourage employees to structure their days in ways that make sense for them. If an employee prefers a mid-day workout or needs to pick up their child from school, that's okay. Productivity isn't tied to the 9-5 anymore.

"I've worked in the People team at a few different companies, but the impact I've seen by implementing a trust-based flexible culture is amazing. Everyone knows they are trusted. If they have an appointment during the day, they'll put in the hours at another time. Everyone really appreciates the autonomy and flexibility".

Hannah Jones, Head of People and Culture at Radar Healthcare.

The Economic Argument: Flexibility as a Competitive Advantage

It's not just about employee satisfaction. On the economic front, flexibility offers tangible benefits that can enhance an organization's competitiveness.

From reduced office costs to access to a broader talent pool unrestricted by geography, the economic advantages of flexibility are significant. This model also allows businesses to be more agile, pivoting in response to market dynamics.

The Flexibility Paradigm

Flexibility is not merely about where and when we work. It's an overarching paradigm shift – redefining productivity, reimagining collaboration, and restructuring organizational priorities. While trends come and go, flexibility is a powerful response to the evolving demands of the modern world. It's more than just a trend; it's the future.

The Freedom of Choice - Unpacking the Modern Workspace

The Evolution of the Workspace

Let's take a little stroll down memory lane. Not too long ago, the definition of 'work' for many was synonymous with a physical location – the office. The rhythm of our days was set by the hum of fluorescent lights, the gentle clatter of keyboard keys, and scheduled coffee breaks.

Fast forward to today, and the landscape is decidedly different. The buzzword is 'choice'. The modern worker isn't just defined by their job title but by where they choose to perform their duties. A dining table might serve as a desk one day, and the next, it's the communal table at the office or a spot at a local coffee shop.

78% of businesses now offer some form of hybrid working, signalling a profound shift in how businesses operate and how employees perceive work.
Chartered Institute of Personnel and Development

Why Choice Matters

Why has choice become such an essential aspect of our work

lives? At its core, it's about autonomy. Having control over one's environment can lead to increased satisfaction and improved performance. Think about it: the freedom to pick a quiet spot for deep work or a collaborative space for team brainstorming can significantly impact productivity and creativity.

Self-Determination Theory, a framework developed by psychologists Richard Ryan and Edward Deci, suggests that people are more motivated and perform better when they feel autonomous. The theory posits that autonomy, competence, and relatedness are the most important factors for human motivation.

Yet, beyond productivity, the power of choice ties deeply into our well-being. Breaking the monotony, experiencing diverse settings, and having the flexibility to align work with personal life can have profound effects on mental health and overall job satisfaction.

Having control over the environment directly correlates to increased satisfaction and efficiency. It's not just about physical comfort but also about psychological well-being. Several studies show that workplace stress is significantly reduced when employees have greater job control. Stress reduction is not just beneficial for mental health but also for physical health, reducing rates of conditions like cardiovascular disease.

"Flexible working has reduced stress, given me more time at my desk, and the ability to work into the evening when necessary. Overall my productivity has improved hugely. Being able to pick and choose when to work in the office gives you more control over your working environment."
Jack Bower, Travel Advisor, One Fine Stay

Navigating the Challenges

Of course, as with any major shift, challenges arise. With the power of choice comes the responsibility of making the right choices. How do we ensure we're in the right place at the right time? How do companies keep a sense of unity when their teams are dispersed? How do you encourage employees to meet up to collaborate and build relationships when they could just stay at home? And finally, how do you know if your expensive office is being used efficiently?

While 78% of companies support flexible workspaces, they also report challenges in maintaining team cohesion and spontaneous collaboration.

Harnessing the Potential

But despite these challenges, the freedom of choice in the workspace is more than a trend; it's a movement. And it's a movement that's here to stay. Next, we'll explore strategies, tools, and insights to ensure that this movement benefits everyone - from the individual employee to the large-scale organization.

The future is not just about remote or office-based work, but a hybrid that combines the best of both worlds.

"We want our team to feel comfortable and inspired, regardless of where they choose to work."
  Jennifer Hollett, Executive Director of The Walrus

The Business Sense Behind Letting Employees Choose Their Workspace

The Real Deal with Choice

When we talk about choice in the workplace, we're really talking about trust. Companies that trust their employees to choose their work environment see it pay off. Why? Because when people have a say in where they work, they naturally gravitate to where they're most effective.

Flexibility isn't just about location but the empowerment that comes with it. It's a nod to the idea that employees, when given autonomy, can make decisions that benefit both themselves and the company.

Studies have indicated that employees with the autonomy to choose their working location have positive effects on overall well-being and higher levels of job satisfaction.
  University of Birmingham

Productivity and Choice: The Dynamic Duo

Every task has its own vibe. Crunching numbers or coding might demand solitude, while brainstorming sessions thrive on energy. Letting employees align their workspace with their tasks isn't just a perk; it's practical. They get to be in their optimal setting, leading to fewer distractions and more work done.

This is because different tasks have varying cognitive demands. Research in cognitive psychology, such as the concept of cognitive load, illustrates how tasks that require deep focus, like data analysis or coding, benefit from solitude and a quiet environment to reduce cognitive strain. Such an environment allows the brain to allocate its processing resources solely to the task at hand, increasing efficiency and reducing errors.

Furthermore, the psychological state known as "flow" is characterized by complete immersion in an activity, leading to heightened productivity and satisfaction. Studies have shown that achieving this state is easier when external conditions align with the demands of the task.

On the other hand, tasks like brainstorming or team meetings often benefit from a more dynamic environment. The theory of group creativity suggests that collaborative settings facilitate the exchange of ideas, leading to more creative outcomes. In such scenarios, the 'buzz' and energy of a group can be conducive to innovation and problem-solving.

Not all people are the same; some are night owls while others are early birds. Some prefer complete silence, others thrive in a coffee shop-like environment. Allowing employees to choose their workspace respects their individual peak performance times and environmental preferences, which has been shown to increase job satisfaction and performance, according to research in occupational health psychology.

When employees are able to work in their optimal settings, they are likely to be more efficient and effective. This leads to quicker task completion and higher-quality work, reducing the need for corrections or rework. In the long run, this translates into cost savings for the organization.

In summary, allowing employees to align their workspace with their tasks isn't just a "nice-to-have"; it's a smart, science-backed strategy that boosts both individual performance and organizational efficiency.

"Switching between home and office depending on my tasks has been a game-changer. I feel more in control of my day and, honestly, I've never been more productive,"
Mike L., *Developer*

Flexibility as a Talent Magnet

The modern workforce values choice. They're drawn to employers who understand the changing dynamics of work and are willing to adapt. Offering workspace flexibility isn't just an HR checkbox; it's a strategic move. It broadcasts a company's forward-thinking nature and respect for individual preferences.

A whopping 75% of millennials and Gen Z employees cite workspace flexibility as a top factor in evaluating job opportunities.
Deloitte

As remote work becomes more common, the narrative shifts from 'remote-friendly' to 'choice-friendly'. Companies that embrace this shift showcase an understanding of evolving work dynamics, setting themselves apart in recruitment and retention.

Being a flexible workplace is evolving into a new standard. Companies that recognize this are not just accommodating their employees; they're strategically positioning themselves to win in the era of flexible work.

"If you're not flexible, you just miss out on so much talent. Think of the number of people who have personal circumstances that mean they can't be in the office on fixed days every week. Whether it be carers or parents, or those with a disability. Why would you want to exclude them from your hiring process?"

Beth Lang, Head of People and Culture, Lunio

Visibility: The Foundation of Effective Flexibility

In the previous chapters, we've ventured through the transformative potential of flexible work. Yet, as we revel in its promises, we confront a significant hiccup: the murkiness of not knowing 'who's where?' and 'who's doing what?'. This chapter is our dive into the power of visibility and how it anchors the ship of flexibility.

A common misconception is that flexibility equals disorder. Some imagine a scene of employees working in isolation, reduced serendipitous interactions, and being unaware of where their teammates are. But flexibility isn't the culprit here—lack of visibility is.

When I started helping companies transition to flexible work, the number 1 problem we faced was making sure employees met up in person. Employees reported fleeing isolated, and our clients felt in-person collaboration, relationships, and the company's overall culture were dwindling.

Often, the knee-jerk reaction was to impose forced office mandates. But we knew how they could blow up in your face. So, we embarked on a fact-finding mission, speaking with as many employees as we could. And we had a remarkable discovery: when asked why they weren't coming into the office, many employees replied that they wanted to come into the office _more_ than they actually were! They said the problem was that they didn't know who would be in the office, if anyone at all, so they didn't want to risk the commute.

This makes sense; why would you spend an hour on public transport or driving in rush hour traffic only to find you are the only one in the office? You might as well have stayed home. This is called commute regret.

This helped us land on the cornerstone of our flexible work strategy: Working Location Visibility.

84% of employees would be motivated to go into the office more by the promise of socializing with co-workers, while 85% would be motivated by rebuilding team bonds. Employees also report that they would go to the office more frequently if they knew their direct team members would be there (73%) or if their work friends were there (74%).
   Microsoft Hybrid Work Study

Clear Visibility, Clear Benefits

As soon as employees get visibility of who is working where each day, office attendance soars. And in doing so, so does in-person collaboration and relationship building, and the office refinds its 'buzz'.

Visibility doesn't just help office attendance. It also helps your teams get back in sync. When we were all working from the office five days a week, we knew if someone was available by just looking over to their desk. But now, colleagues can be anywhere. They could be working from home, visiting a client, travelling for work or off on vacation. This breakdown in knowing teammates' availability can cause huge inefficiencies in the output of your employees. Get them back in sync.

The benefits of visibility:

- **Fostering Collaboration:** When you know your marketing expert is working from the downtown hub, you can join them for a brainstorming session.
- **Building Relationships:** When employees can see that their team and work friends are in the office on Wednesday, they are excited to go in and not miss out on the fun.
- **Avoiding Commute Regret:** Your employees aren't going to risk commuting into the office only to find they are the only ones in. Visibility encourages higher office attendance.
- **Strengthening Culture:** Celebrating a teammate's birthday or a project milestone? With visibility, spontaneous meetups or celebrations become easier to organize, making everyone feel involved and valued.
- **Efficient Resource Allocation:** Need a meeting room or desk? Knowing who's where helps optimize resource usage, ensuring no double bookings or resource clashes.

"Visibility is key. If everyone knows where everyone is working, your team can be intentional about meeting up to build relationships and

to collaborate. We show our working location in our Slack Status and in our calendar. Officely is great for this."
Freya McDonnell, People Operations Manager, nPlan

Predictability in Flexibility: The Power of Forecasting

Flexibility comes with patterns, sometimes subtle, sometimes overt. Discerning these patterns allows teams and managers to anticipate needs, ensuring seamless operations. Recognizing when the office buzzes with energy versus when remote collaborations peak can guide various decisions, such as:

- Streamlining resource distribution, ensuring offices and resources aren't overwhelmed.
- Organizing team-building or training sessions when most members prefer an in-office setting.
- Adjusting support staff and resources based on predicted office attendance.

The Trust Factor: Empowering Without Micromanaging

True empowerment lies in trusting employees to make the best decisions for themselves and the company.

Visibility tools aren't surveillance mechanisms but trust enablers. By granting employees the freedom to choose and having systems that transparently reflect those choices, companies create an environment of mutual respect. Such a setting yields benefits like:

- Enhanced job satisfaction as employees feel valued and

trusted.
- A self-motivated workforce keen on proving their commitment.
- Reduced friction between management and teams, fostering a more cohesive working environment.

"It makes me feel like my company respects us as adults, and is not being too restrictive. Makes for a more positive working environment."
Jack Bower, One Fine Stay

Beyond the Now: Using Visibility for Future Growth

Visibility isn't just a momentary glimpse but a continuous story, hinting at broader trends and possibilities. By paying attention to these patterns, companies can:

- Foresee and act upon emerging work trends before they become mainstream.
- Strategically expand, choosing new locations or remote hubs based on consistent data.
- Refine and evolve their flexibility models to cater to future workforce needs.

Tools for Enhanced Visibility

To truly embrace flexible work, companies need to invest in tools that provide this crucial visibility. It's not about tracking or micromanaging—it's about understanding team dynamics in real-time, ensuring everyone is in sync.

The Future is Visible

As we propel forward in this era of flexible work, visibility will be the anchor that ensures fluidity doesn't turn into chaos. It's the key to unlocking the true potential of a flexible, modern workspace.

Remember: Flexibility doesn't mean working in the dark. It's about shining a light on where and how we work best.

"When we asked our team what would make them want to come into the office more, they said just knowing who else would be there."
Nina Gordon, Culture and Communications Lead, Pleo

Flexibility is Not Chaos

Demystifying Flexibility: Choice, Not Chance

Flexibility in the workspace isn't about leaving things to fate; it's about empowering choices.

Multiple research studies underline a singular truth: when employees are given the autonomy to choose their work environment, their engagement and productivity levels soar. This isn't about unsupervised freedom; it's structured autonomy, built on trust.

"Adopting flexible work at our organization wasn't about throwing the rulebook out the window. It was about rewriting it together. My personal productivity peaks between 10 AM and 6 PM, and I've tailored my day around that."
Sam D., Developer.

Setting Boundaries: The Framework of Flexibility

But freedom without boundaries is a recipe for chaos. That's why successful flexibility is built on a foundation of clear guidelines and expectations.

Successful companies often delineate 'core hours' for collaborative tasks or empower team managers to be able to pull everyone into the office for team building and collaboration. By offering a combination of freedom and structure, organizations ensure a harmonious balance between individual needs and team cohesion.

Designing a "Flexibility Charter" can be a great way for organizations to outline the do's and don'ts of flexible working, ensuring everyone is on the same page.

The Two-Way Street: Empowerment and Responsibility

With the freedom of choice comes the onus of responsibility on your employees. Flexibility shines when it is backed by accountability.

It's not just about where you work but how effectively you do so. Clear objectives, regular check-ins, and transparent communication are pivotal. Tools that offer visibility into tasks and timelines become invaluable in such setups.

Platforms like Asana or Trello provide transparent tracking of tasks and milestones. They're not just accountability tools but also mediums to celebrate team achievements.

Technology: The Unseen Bridge of Flexibility

While flexibility is about people and choices, technology is the silent enabler, making it all possible without a hitch.

Today's digital tools facilitate communication, collaboration, and camaraderie, ensuring that physical distance doesn't translate into professional disconnect. They replicate the office's collaborative spirit in the virtual realm.

"Our design team is spread over four continents. Yet, with the right tech stack, brainstorming feels as interactive and spontaneous as if we were in the same room."
Miguel V., Design Lead.

Embrace tools like Slack for communication, Miro for brainstorming, Zoom for face-to-face interactions, and of course, Officely for working location visibility. These tools don't replace the office; they extend its boundaries.

Structured Flexibility - The Future's Blueprint

The journey from traditional workspaces to a flexible model isn't about discarding the old but refining it. By blending choice with structure, organizations are not just adopting a trend; they're architecting the future of work.

Why Office Mandates Don't Work

The office—once a symbol of professionalism, collaboration, and structured routine. But as the world evolved, our perspective on work has shifted. We've tasted flexibility, experienced the perks of personalized work environments, and reaped the benefits of a work-life balance that doesn't hinge on a daily commute.

The Illusion of Control

Many organizations, in an attempt to bring back some semblance of the 'old normal,' have reintroduced office mandates. They've painted them as necessary for fostering collaboration, preserving company culture, or enhancing productivity. But what they often miss is that these mandates are mere illusions of control.

Forced Presence ≠ Productivity. Being physically present in an office doesn't guarantee efficiency. In fact, it can often introduce distractions—unnecessary meetings, casual chatter, or the simple discomfort of a non-personalized workspace.

One Size Doesn't Fit All

Today's workforce is a rich tapestry of skills, backgrounds, and lifestyles. From caregiving responsibilities to evening courses, people's personal commitments vary widely. Office mandates often fail to accommodate this diversity, stifling personal growth and professional development. Moreover, different job roles have distinct needs for optimal productivity. For instance, research suggests that roles requiring deep focus, such as software engineering, benefit from a distraction-free environment often found at home. In contrast, collaborative roles like sales and project management thrive on the spontaneity and social support that an office can provide.

But work demands are fluid, changing from day to day and even week to week. One week might call for the social hustle of office meetings, while the next requires focused at-home work to finalize a project. Adding to the complexity is the fact that individuals have their own circadian rhythms and peak performance times. Whether you're a morning person who prefers the quiet dawn hours at home or a night owl who thrives in the evening, a rigid office schedule can be a significant constraint.

By acknowledging these diverse needs and allowing for a more flexible, choice-driven work environment, organizations can better align with the scientific insights and real-world demands that drive modern productivity.

"Mandates feel like a violation of autonomy, which is one of the most important intrinsic drivers of threat and reward in the brain."
David Rock and Christy Pruitt-Haynes, Harvard Business Review

Missing Out on Talent

Office mandates can be a significant barrier to accessing the best talent available. The modern workplace is becoming increasingly global, thanks in part to the technological advances that make remote work not just possible. When companies insist on local hires who can come into an office every day, they're unwittingly restricting themselves to a smaller talent pool.

Think about it: the person who could take your project to the next level might be sitting in a coffee shop halfway around the world, armed with skills you can't find locally. When you require employees to be in the office, you lose out on this person—and countless others with diverse skill sets, perspectives, and experiences that can enrich your company.

Moreover, international talent can provide insights into markets that you might be looking to expand into, offering cultural and localized understanding that you can't get from a domestic team. They can also work around the clock if they are in a different time zone, essentially enabling a 24/7 operation without requiring anyone to work night shifts.

By removing the geographical boundaries through flexible work arrangements, companies can tap into global expertise, resulting in a more innovative, diverse, and effective workforce. It's not just about filling roles; it's about accessing the minds that could drive your company forward, no matter where they happen to be located.

"If you're not flexible, you just miss out on so much talent. Think of the number of people who have personal circumstances that mean they can't be in the office on fixed days every week. Whether it be

carers or parents, or those with a disability. Why would you want to exclude them from your hiring process?"
Beth Lang, Head of People and Culture, Lunio

Employee Churn and Recruitment Challenges

In a job market where candidates are increasingly looking for work-life balance and autonomy, rigid office mandates can act as a deterrent for top talent. Research shows that a lack of flexibility can be a major deal-breaker for potential employees. According to a study by McKinsey, 21% of workers are moving jobs because of not being offered flexible work options, whereas in the UK, an estimated 4 million people have changed careers due to the lack of flexible work opportunities, according to CIPD.

Beyond the recruitment phase, office mandates can also contribute to higher employee turnover. A study published in the Journal of Vocational Behavior found that job dissatisfaction stemming from inflexible work conditions is one of the significant predictors of turnover intentions. Employees who find themselves struggling to balance personal responsibilities, such as caregiving or education, with rigid office hours are more likely to seek out employers who offer more accommodating work environments.

Not only does higher turnover result in the loss of skilled employees, but it's also expensive for businesses. The cost of employee turnover can be substantial—ranging from 16% to 213% of the lost employee's salary, depending on the role and level of the employee, according to the Center for American

Progress. These costs include hiring, onboarding, training, ramp time to peak productivity, and the loss of engagement from others due to high turnover.

Moreover, in an age where employer branding is crucial, high employee churn rates can harm a company's reputation, making it even more challenging to attract quality talent. According to Glassdoor, 69% of job seekers would not take a job with a company that has a bad reputation, even if unemployed, which goes to show the significance of employee satisfaction and its impact on recruitment.

It's in the best interest of organizations to reconsider office mandates and embrace more flexible work options if they want to attract and retain top talent in today's competitive job market.

Finding a Middle Ground

It's not about completely shunning the office, but rather understanding its new role. The office can be a hub—a place for occasional meetups, intensive collaboration sessions, or simply a change of environment for those who seek it.

- Trust Over Surveillance: Trusting employees to manage their schedules and tasks can yield better results than micromanaging their office hours.
- Redefining Purpose: Instead of a mandate, organizations can redefine the purpose of their office spaces, making them more flexible, welcoming, and suited for sporadic visits.

As the lines between work and life continue to blur, flexibility is no longer a luxury—it's a necessity. Office mandates, in their rigid, one-size-fits-all approach, are not just outdated, but counterproductive. The future is flexible, and organizations that recognize this will lead the charge in innovation, productivity, and employee satisfaction.

"Your employees know how best to deliver. You just need to show that you trust them. If they need to focus, they'll likely work from home. If they need to collaborate, they'll likely go into the office. Only they know where they will be most productive on each day."
Freya McDonnell, People Operations Manager, nPlan

Data-Driven Insights Amplify Flexibility's Potential

Beyond Gut Feelings: The Role of Data in Flexibility

While instincts have their place, modern workspaces can't thrive on intuition alone. Enter the era of data, the silent guide in the flexible work journey.

Gone are the days of trial and error. With advanced analytical tools, organizations can make informed decisions about their flexible work strategies. From gauging employee satisfaction and tracking peak productivity hours to evaluating the efficacy of the office, data provides invaluable insights.

"We need to make sure we're maximizing any investment into office space effectively. Some of our offices we'll downsize, other times we'll need to upscale. If we see an office is at full capacity every day, it's time to look at alternative spaces."
Maria Fuster, Workplace Operations Lead, Adaptavist

Personalized Flexibility: Tailoring Workspaces Through

Analytics

The beauty of flexibility lies in its uniqueness. Data helps in deciphering individual preferences to create an environment that feels tailor-made.

Each employee is an individual, and data analytics can unravel their unique work patterns. Is there a specific day of the week when office occupancy peaks? Do some employees prefer collaborative sessions on a Wednesday? Does your office need to be so big? Or do certain events or certain people coming into the office result in increased attendance? Analytics offer answers to these questions, allowing for a more bespoke approach to flexibility and the ability to plan ahead.

"Data helped us realize that when senior managers travelled in from our New York Office, attendance soared. So we now arrange team events when they are in town."
Nina R., Office Experience Lead.

The Cycle of Evolution: Data's Role in Continuous Adaptation

In the ever-evolving landscape of flexible workspaces, stagnation isn't an option. Data ensures that organizations remain adaptive, relevant, and efficient.

Flexible work models should be fluid, continuously adapting to new challenges and opportunities. By regularly revisiting metrics, reassessing strategies, and iterating based on feedback, companies can ensure that their flexible models remain at the forefront of efficiency.

Navigating the Future with Data

In the maze of flexibility, data acts as the guiding light, ensuring that organizations remain not just reactive, but proactive in their approach. When flexibility is fused with data-driven insights, the result is a workspace that's not only modern but also efficient, inclusive, and ever-evolving.

Managing Employees in a Flexible Workplace

The New Age of Autonomy: Trust Over Surveillance

In the age of the flexible workspace, a new management paradigm has taken root. The lens of micromanagement, which may have been the norm in traditional office environments, doesn't quite fit here. Flexible workspaces shift the balance, emphasizing trust over surveillance.

The modern workspace recognizes that employees are not just cogs in a machine; they're dynamic individuals who crave autonomy. Micromanaging, with its constant surveillance and control, is not just counterproductive but could also harm morale. In contrast, trust generates respect, deepens commitment, and fosters innovation. Trusting employees to manage their schedules and choose their work environments is now non-negotiable.

61% of employees reported that they would prefer if they were allowed to come into the office when they need to and work from home when they need to. In other words, it's conditional upon autonomy.
   Jabra Hybrid Work Study

A Two-Way Street: Feedback and Open Channels

Empowerment isn't simply about granting freedom and stepping back. It's a continuous conversation, a partnership between the employer and the employee. In the world of flexible workspaces, feedback isn't just useful; it's vital.

Being responsive to the shifting needs and concerns of employees ensures that the flexible models provided stay agile, effective, and relevant. This continuous dialogue makes employees feel integral to the decision-making process, enhancing their sense of belonging. Furthermore, this feedback loop can unveil hidden challenges and open doors to innovative solutions.

Regular feedback sessions, facilitated by digital platforms, can provide insights into employees' evolving needs. And anonymous surveys can be a powerful tool in capturing unfiltered feedback.

"You need to understand what your employees want from flexible work, and what they value in an office, and then provide that."
Nina Gordon, Culture and Communications Lead, Pleo

Celebrating Successes: Recognition in the Flexible Era

The digital realm may have changed how we work, but the human need for recognition remains unchanged. It's the glue that binds teams, fostering motivation and camaraderie.

Recognition in the flexible workspace era must be innovative. It's about translating physical acknowledgements—like a pat on the back or a round of applause in a meeting—into digital equivalents that resonate just as profoundly. This shift might mean virtual shoutouts, digital badges, or unique recognition rituals that the team can look forward to.

Use platforms like Bonusly or Kudos to infuse recognition into everyday workflow seamlessly. Even if it's a digital badge or a shoutout in a team chat, the impact of these gestures is profound.

The Empowerment Ecosystem

Empowerment isn't an isolated act; it's an ecosystem. An ecosystem where trust, feedback, skill development, and recognition feed into each other, creating a vibrant, motivated, and efficient workspace. This empowerment ecosystem doesn't just bolster productivity; it builds a culture. A culture where every individual knows their worth, feels valued, and is motivated to contribute their best.

The Path Forward with Flexibility at its Core

Reflecting on Flexibility's Power

The journey through the evolving landscape of the working world has underscored the profound transformation flexible work brings. It represents a blend of employee autonomy with organizational dynamism.

Historically, work was limited by physical boundaries. From the confines of factories to the cubicles of offices, workspaces dictated workflows. Now, the digital era has freed us from these chains. Flexibility is not just about working from home; it's about untethering work from place.

Flexible work models aren't just employee perks; they're strategic masterstrokes. They foster an environment that encourages adaptability, resilience, and innovative thinking. For organizations, embracing flexibility means not just staying relevant, but leading the charge into the future.

"As a new parent, it's difficult to imagine how different my life would be without flexible work. If I had to be in the office five days a week, the extra load I'd have to put onto my already stretched wife would

be immense, not to mention the hours I'd lose with my daughter."
Max Shepherd-Cross, CEO Officely

Gazing into the Future: The Boundless Potential of Flexibility

The flexible future is not bound by four walls. It's expansive, uncharted, and bursting with potential.

As we move ahead, we can anticipate even more technological innovations that further dissolve geographical barriers, making collaborations seamless and instantaneous. The future workspace is not a place but a network of digital connections.

By 2025, some predict that we might have virtual reality meetings, making remote collaborations as immersive as in-person ones. With advancements in AI, routine tasks could be automated, allowing humans to focus on creative and strategic aspects of their roles.

The Collective Call: Every Individual's Role in Shaping the Future

While the onus of shaping flexible work models might seem to lie with organizational leaders, it's a collective endeavour. Each stakeholder, from the freshest intern to the most seasoned executive, holds a piece of this puzzle.

As employees, it's vital to invest in self-management skills and continuous learning. In a world where autonomy is a given, discipline becomes crucial.

Final Thoughts: The Road Ahead

Flexible work has the potential to be the most significant upgrade in the quality of our working lives we experience in our lifetimes. But its success is far from guaranteed. There are still companies and executives enforcing office mandates, and a recent study has found that 64% of leaders think we'll be back in the office five days a week by 2026.

So, let this be your rallying cry. Let's not return to the way things were. Let's make Flexible Work, really work.

If you have any questions, please get in touch max@getofficely.com

Printed in Great Britain
by Amazon